SOCIAL MEDIA SUCCESS:

30 Strategies

To Boost Your

Online Business

By

A.C. Jones

Other books by A.C. Jones:

10 Ways to Make $1000 Online

More Life, Less Work: 45 Simple Strategies to Achieve Maximum Productivity and Success

Table of Contents

Introduction

Social media has become a part of everyone's lives, businesses included. Statistics show that 72% of adults in North America use social media. Having access to that 72% of the population is priceless for business marketing. However, just because they are utilizing social media, does not mean that they are looking at you. As a business, you need to know how to stand out on social media to attract their attention.

In this book, we will look at 30 different strategies to boost your online business. The strategies will be based off of some of the most popular social media networks. Such as:

1. Facebook
2. LinkedIn
3. Pinterest
4. YouTube
5. Twitter

Each one presents different opportunities to grab an audience's attention. We will see how different strategies can provide benefits to your business marketing, such as:

1. Building a reputation for your business
2. Building strong and long lasting relationships with your customers
3. Engaging your customers
4. Increasing your sales
5. Finding repeat customers
6. Becoming an expert in your industry
7. Brand recognition

It's important to know how to grab people's attention, but it's also important to discover what NOT to do. Social media is a community. Each community has unstated rules that businesses and users need to follow. If you do not follow those rules, you risk creating a bad reputation. You risk losing the audience you once had. In this book we will identify those habits to avoid.

Regardless of what platform you select for your social networking, you will need to understand what it takes to succeed. All content must be focused on keywords so that your audience can find the information they need. You will want to take advantage of all of the different audiences and link them together. Make sure that your profiles are connected and that a person can easily find your other profiles if they want. It's also important to analyze any strategy you use to make sure it is working for you.

1. Create a Great Brand Page on Facebook

A brand page is different than a personal page on Facebook. They offer incentives like activity, integration, communication, and the ability for advertising. If you make your brand page interesting enough, the activity can become your online business. Facebook is great at integrating with other types of social media. The different sites can be linked together and increase visibility, while allowing you to communicate with your friends and customers.

It is important to make sure that your brand page is humanized. It should be something that people can relate to. You will need to avoid having a page that looks too formal. This can be achieved through your posts. Talk as if you were really talking. Do not state things in an awkward fashion. Remember that Facebook is about connecting with people. You will drive people away if you try and shove product down their throat. Find a way to reward your fans for showing up to your page. Offer them special deals or highlight a post about them. Consider showing content from behind the scenes. This will help them relate to what you are doing.

1. Start a brand page by selecting 'Create a Page' for your business in the left hand column.
2. The site will ask you to select an applicable category. There is a selection of local businesses, artistic, bands, public figures, companies, organizations, institutions, entertainment, brands, products, or community causes.
3. Complete all of the profile information. Include information regarding your business hours and contact information. When you enter your company name and your location, remember that you cannot change these. If you need to change them, it will require deleting the page and starting from scratch.
4. Select a main photo that will be displayed on your posts and comments. It will appear as a small icon. Most people like to choose a logo to make it recognizable to

customers. The photo will need to shrink to 125x125 pixels.

5. Complete the "About" section. You'll want to find 2-3 sentences that explain what your company is about. Include a link to your website at the beginning.
6. Customize things by using the Admin Panel. You can change company information, manage the pages administrators, and manage notifications. Let Facebook help you build an audience for your brand page. This includes inviting contacts, fans, and users. Remember to include your personal friends. Make sure that the page is completed to your liking before inviting people.
7. Find the perfect cover photo. This picture is the best real estate on your Facebook brand page. You might also want to place text in the photo to communicate your message more clearly to your fans.

Your posts on your brand page are important. They are the way you are going to connect to your fans and friends. You will want to remain humanized. Make sure that you respond to everyone and make sure to respond to both good and bad comments.

Acknowledging the bad will show customers that you are trustworthy and also respectable. Be sure to tell them exactly what you want. If you want them to visit your site, ask them too. Keep your posts regular and relevant and avoid getting too pitchy.

Some successful businesses also choose to plan their posts ahead of time, using software such as Hootsuite. You can also limit the amount of text you put into your posts and remember that the shorter it is, the posts get more attention. If the site cuts you off, it's too long.

2. Utilize Facebook Boosted Posts

A boosted post is the same as a regular post. It extends the reach of people that the post gets to. It's great for businesses because it allows you to target an audience handpicked from the type of business that you have. You can choose the age or location of the people that would benefit from seeing your post the most.

Start by creating a post. At the bottom right of the post an option will be visible that says, "Boost Post". This will only show up after a post has received 100 or more "likes" from your audience. Click the button. Facebook will give you options to target an audience. You can select to have your post limited to your friends and their friends. You can also choose to target people through other options. Select the drop down menu for the "add targeting".

Then you simply select options that suit your business by location, age, gender, or even language. Finally, decide what your budget is. Enter that amount. Facebook will estimate how many people should see your ad. It has been noted that this may not be accurate. Yet, it will get you a general idea of what a difference you're targeting selections and budget will make.

What to Avoid in a Targeted Post

Be careful not to boost a post that takes a person to someone else's page. When you select to view it if you choose the friends of your friends, you may be wasting the effort. Just because the people are extensions of your contacts, does not mean that they have an interest in the same things. It may be wasted exposure.

When you decide to boost a post, it will show up in people's newsfeed. The budget that you placed on the post can be from $5 to several hundred. You need to make sure that your post is worth reading and liking. Your post should be used to expand your audience and promote the validity of your business. Ultimately, your post should increase the amount of views you receive.

There are some guidelines that need to be met for a post to be boosted. The post has to already have the 100 "likes" needed. It is also important to understand the relationship between images and texts in your post. You will need to have less than 20% text with an image for it to be accepted. Otherwise, Facebook may reject it. It's also important to understand that for every account, you can only run one boosted post at a time.

Finding an audience for your online business requires being visible. Facebook is a great method of making that happen. A boosted post may require a little bit of money, but it benefits a business owner by extending the reach of people beyond what is already capable. You have the ability to reach out to your friends' friends. You can also reach out to a specific group of audience that may benefit from seeing your post. There are also certain limitations to your post that can be learned and understood.

3. Create a Facebook Promoted Post

We talked about creating boosted posts for your online business. The next step up in strategies would be a promoted post. It allows someone to increase their reach in audience. There are however, certain things that should be avoided when using these posts. It's also important to understand the requirements for the posts.

An online business will want to use a promoted post to increase their engagement with their followers. It is a budget friendly option to promote your brand. If it is used properly, you can increase your brand awareness. It is different than a boosted post because you have more targeting options for your audience. There are also more options for how you pay for your promotion.

When you promote a post, you want to make sure that it is a post that will stand out in a newsfeed. This is where your viewers are going to see your post. Any image that is used can only be accompanied with 20% or less text. Therefore, it's important to select the words you use carefully. Make each one count. That text will only be promoted for 3 days. Once you promote a post, it cannot be stopped until the time runs out. Your post will be seen with a sponsored tag viewed on the corner of it.

Once a post has been up for at least 6 hours, you can select the "Promote" option on it. You can allow the post to be viewed by your friends and your friends' friends. If you want to go further, it requires payment. You can narrow down the Facebook audience by location, age, gender, and language. After deciding that you want to pay for the promotion, you will need to determine if you want to run the post with a daily budget or with a cost per click amount.

The content of the post is important. You want to pick the right one to promote so that your efforts are not wasted. Start out with a small budget and see how your post does. You can increase the amount of payment after sampling that it is worth the money. Make sure that you do not have time sensitive information within the post that will be irrelevant within 3 days. The post will be promoted for the full 3 days and you would not want to waste the efforts when the information is no longer relevant during the campaign. Find a way to include a call of action for the viewers. Ask them to do whatever it is you want them to. If you want them to check out your website, say so. Also, make sure that the post you select to promote has at least a 1% engagement rate already. People should already be commenting and liking the post without the promotion.

You can access Facebook's Ads Reports area to see a report of your post before and after the campaign. You also have the benefit of being seen on Facebook's mobile app. Facebook ads and sponsored stories are not visible on the mobile app.

Facebook promoted posts offer an extended reach of visibility to an online business. There are more payment options than a boosted post. The visibility extends beyond the typical program and can be seen on mobile applications as well. It will help to gain momentum in brand recognition for any business.

4. Create Facebook Offers

Creating a Facebook Offer on Facebook is great for any online business. It gives the advantage of building mailing lists. It will help to draw attention to your brand and build brand recognition. If used properly, Facebook offers can create a surge in the amount of viewing and interaction for any business.

Here's how to get started creating the perfect offer:

1. Start by clicking on "Offer, Event, +" at the top of your brand page.
2. Select the option, "Offer".
3. Enter your information. Be sure to complete it 100%. You will need the name of your offer. Find a proper description with details of your deal. Select any images that you would want to include. Decide on an expiration date for the offer. Decide upon the audience you want to reach. Narrow the Facebook audience down by location, cities, and age. Enter in the budget you determine that's available. Facebook will complete it by estimating the amount of people that the offer will receive.
4. You will be able to select more options after entering the basic information. You can give your offer a start date. Decide if you want an online redemption link. Also, you have the ability to select and outline your terms and conditions.
5. On the top left of your page, you will see a preview of your offer. Take a look at it and make sure that it will stand out. You want your offer to be inviting, warm and humanized. Be careful not to come off as too pushy.
6. Finalize your offer by clicking, "Create Offer".

Creating an offer on Facebook is free. If you want to increase the amount of people it reaches, you will need to promote it. Promoting an offer will require a budget.

A successful offer should have certain aspects in it. You will need to offer substantial discounts. It's important that you have at least 20% off or something for free. Your terms should be simple. Your fans and friends don't want to take part in something that takes too much thinking. The image that you select should be something that personalizes the offer. Photos of people using the product are better than someone showcasing the product alone.

These photos are better than including a logo. The logo should appear on your brand page and as your icon. It's also important that any image you use looks good at the smaller size. Your headline should include the offer value. The expiration date should be reasonable. It's also important to create an ad for the offer and pin it to your brand page.

Keep track of your offer and make sure that it is performing well. At the bottom of your brand timeline, you will see the Page Insights. The offer will also list the amount of views at the bottom corner.

Finding the right Facebook offer will help to jumpstart an audience and fan base for any online business. It will increase the number of new customers. The increase in word of mouth is priceless. Those that decide to share your offer will help to reach out even further. The use of Facebook offers also for allows greater tracking ability.

5. Create a Facebook Ad

Facebook Ads are another method of extending the reach of your online business. If used correctly, you will be able to gain recognition of your brand. You will be able to find customers in places that may not be otherwise accessible. Creating a Facebook ad will help to boost your online business.

When you create a Facebook ad, the users that see your ad are selected according to their previous page likes, their web searches and the applications that they use. This will help to ensure that the people seeing your information will value it.

1. Start creating a Facebook ad by using the Create Advert tool.
2. You will need to select an objective for your ad. Choose from gaining clicks, conversions, page likes, offer claims or responses to events. Facebook will target users that are most likely to help you reach your objective.
3. Choose the image and text that you want to use in your ad. Keep the image pleasant to look at. It should stand out in a newsfeed in a positive way. You don't want to annoy people with its presence. You can use up to 6 images without adding additional costs. Images will show up in the newsfeed at 600x225 pixels. Therefore, it's important to make sure that the image looks good at that size. Your ad should include no more than 20% text.
4. A preview of the ad will show up to the right.
5. Narrow down the audience that your ad will target. There are much more categories to narrow down the audience rather than boosted or promoted posts. You can select locations, age, gender, interests, categories and different connections.
6. Change the campaign name to something that is meaningful to you.

7. Select your budget along with the start and end date of your ad.
8. Choose the payment option you want to use.

Our Facebook ad should include a great headline. It will be the most important aspect of your ad. You will need to include your brand page as the landing page for your ad.   When you create your ad, keep in mind that people are on Facebook for the purpose of connecting. They do not want products shoved down their throat. This is important for keeping visibility and not becoming a nuisance.

There are different ways to be successful through Facebook ads. One method that works well is to create multiple ads. Start with a small budget and put them out there in small amounts. Give them a small amount of time to find what ads are performing well. Once an ad is highlighted as being a good performer, you can increase the amount of promotion for that ad. This will help to make sure that your budget is used wisely.

Facebook ads are a great way to reach out to a very selective audience. Each view of your ad will be selected based on their actions. The increase in engagement should occur relatively quickly with the right ad and the right budget.

6. Know What to Avoid on Facebook

Facebook is great for online businesses. It reaches out to so many people. You can increase your brand recognition. You can offer discounts, deals, and word of expertise to so many that you ordinarily would not have access to. Facebook is a wonderful tool when used correctly. However, there are ways to misuse Facebook.

Here is a list of what not to do when using Facebook:

1. **Do not block comments.** Some businesses use this technique because they are worried that people may post negative responses. However, by allowing customers the freedom of their responses, you are showing that you are open to communicating with them. You can gain their respect and trust by professionally addressing any negative comments.

2. **Do not abandon your page.** Every comment, like, or share should be addressed. People will forget about a page that has not been updated regularly.

3. **Do not use your personal page for promoting your online business.** Take advantage of the specific perks that a Facebook brand page has to offer. Brand pages will show customers that you are serious about your product. It will also allow you the usage of Analytics to evaluate how your page is functioning for your business.

4. **Do not use Groups to spread word of mouth.** Search engines will penalize you for this. It's important to find a way to reach out to individuals instead.

5. **Do not post too often.** You want to be present in their newsfeed, but not obnoxious.

6. **Avoid hashtags. Hashtags are known for Twitter.** Search engines will recognize that you are using multiple social media sites for promotional value and may penalize you for it.

7. **Do not treat a page like a profile.** Keep the content relevant to your customers and friends of the brand. Remember that personal information should be saved for your personal page.

8. **Do not use your brand page for promotional material only.** Once you have created these connections, share relevant information with them. No one on Facebook is there to have product and services shoved down their throats. They have an interest in your product, but also in the relevant topic that your product addresses. Become an expert on your product and the category for your customers and fans.

9. **Do not overuse text in your postings.** People tend to ignore lengthy posts. They should not have to click to read more of your post. Keep your posts short and sweet.

10. **Do not talk AT your customers.** You need to find a way to talk with your customers instead of at them. Talking AT your customers means that it is one sided. You are giving information without the anticipation of any response or feedback. Talking with them is

engaging them in conversation that benefits from feedback and response.

11. **Do not bad mouth the competition.** If you provide a better service, that will speak to your customers without having to say the words. Engaging in bad mouthing competition can annoy your customers and burn bridges that you may need one day.

12. **Do not post without checking for spelling and grammar.** Show that you are serious about your business and that you would never settle for lessening the quality.

13. **Do not use all capital letters.** It may be that your CAPS LOCK button is on. However, it looks like you are yelling at your customers. No one wants to be yelled at.

Facebook is great for connecting to people. However, it is easy to send a bad message to those people about your company if you do not know exactly how to act on Facebook.

7. Take a Passive Approach on LinkedIn

LinkedIn is the leading social media site for business to business connections. It is also great for connecting with others within the same industry. An online business can connect with other experts in their field to show their dedication to the industry. They can keep up to date with businesses behind the scene. LinkedIn can help businesses to gain exposure.

Taking a passive approach means that you just let the customers and the businesses come to you. These will be people searching for your services or your business. They are actively seeking what you have to give. If you do not have the profile created, you will miss out on the opportunity of being there for those customers. Make no mistake, someone else will be. Therefore, you just handed business to the competitors. Create your profile and make it stand out against the competition to help those that need it.

Start by creating a profile. Complete all the information that the site will allow you. Then, you need to look for connections. They can be people that you have worked with, those that are experts in your topic, or businesses that you collaborate with. The act of connecting with these businesses will give you access to further connections.

Your LinkedIn home page will contain a lot of information about your business. You will need to select a cover photo. If there are any company updates, they will be displayed on your page. Find products and services that you would recommend and create links to those businesses for your customers. Provide your home page with a great description of your company. Use your page to sell products and services. Link the most important of products first and continue to add on. Follow up those products by asking for people to review them.

Your cover photo is important to attracting people to your profile. It needs to be visually appealing. A great bonus is to include some descriptive words about your business in the picture. You will also want a recognizable logo on your profile.

Creating a LinkedIn page allows your profile to build its own promotional activity. It will bring awareness to your brand. You will improve your credibility thought the connections you make and the reviews you receive. It will also allow you the possibility of increasing word of mouth about your business. So, start your LinkedIn profile now.

8. Utilize LinkedIn Groups

LinkedIn has great groups to help find the perfect potential customers. It will also help to engage current customers. The groups can be joined or you can create your own group. The important thing to remember is that this is a way to connect with your customers, not sell to them. The random directing to a product may be ok in small doses, but you want to find a way to make yourself an expert on the product or service instead.

Using your LinkedIn page, you can search for relevant groups. Keep the topic relevant to your online business. It's ok to join as many groups as you want. However, to make a quality reputation for your business, select the top 5-10 and focus on them. When you conduct your search, use the keywords that you would use within your online business.

Why Join a LinkedIn Group?

Joining a LinkedIn group allows you to view the members within the group. You can also see the similar groups that they are involved in. LinkedIn will suggest similar groups to you that you should check out. Consider looking at your customers' LinkedIn pages and seeing the groups that they belong to.

Once you find the groups they belong to, you will want to create relevant content to share. Make sure that you are contributing. You can use blog posts, articles, guides, or expert advice and answers to discussion questions. Stay away from throwing promotional material into the mix. You can direct them to your site if there are answers there for the problems. Otherwise, people will become annoyed at the promotional tactic and you will miss the opportunity to use the group to build your reputation. Contact and connect with group members to help them know who you are.

You can also build your own group on LinkedIn. You will need to know how to manage it appropriately. It will take more work than joining someone else's group. When you name the group, make sure that the name is relevant to your online business. There is a lot you can do with a group that is made up of people interested in your topic. Consider asking a question and polling the answers. Use the group to test out an idea or gain feedback about something. Post information about products and ask them to review them.

In your group, you will want to personally approve and welcome all registrants. You can send them an email. In the email, you will want to let them know how to contact you. Keep constant communication with the group. Go out and search for likely members and invite them. Don't always wait for people to come to you. If your members have something worth celebrating, do it with them. Begin open-ended discussions for everyone to take part in. There will be those that start off-topic conversations. Find an appropriate place for these and direct them there. Use other methods of engaging them, such as telecasts, webinars and online chats.

Using a LinkedIn group can help get your customers engaged in your topic. If you declare and prove that you are the expert in your field, the connection will naturally move on to your business. Be sure to invite your customers to your LinkedIn group. Share your business content within your group. However, be careful not to let it be pushy sales content.

LinkedIn groups are a great way of reaching out to those interested in the topic of your online business. The members have the opportunity to recommend you and to connect with you as an expert on the topic. You can join an already existing group or create your own. Either method has a lot of possibility in growing your online business network.

9. Using Skills Endorsement Feature on LinkedIn

LinkedIn has a feature to show off a business of person's skill set. This is Skills and Endorsements. You are responsible for selecting the skills that your business possesses. Any friend, member, or fan can then endorse that skill. Endorsing skills means that they have witnessed that you are an expert in that skill. Skill endorsements may be the one thing that sets you apart from the competition. You may select a skill that is more detailed or out of the box than the competition.

Using the skills and endorsements is great for building credibility. It brings strength and expertise to your brand name. The increase in connection with your friends, members, or fans only engages your audience even more.

There are two ways to go about getting more endorsements. You can simply ask in a polite manner for customers, friends, fans, or members to endorse those skills. You can also start off by endorsing others. There's a pretty good chance that when you endorse someone for their skills, they will return the favor.

In order to receive endorsements, you will need to scroll to your "Skills and Endorsement" section. This will list all the endorsements that you have already received. Keep in mind that a skill cannot be deleted. It can be hidden. You can add any skill that you want. The more endorsements you receive, the more credible your business will look. The amount of endorsements you receive may be the thing that separates you from the competition. When someone endorses your skills, acknowledge it with an email or some form of contact.

If you want to give an endorsement, know that you are building stronger connections. It is a way of showing support to coworkers, members, friends, and others. It is also a handy tool to begin dialogue with that person. Endorsements can lead to recommendations. Don't be afraid to ask someone who endorsed you to post a small note of recommendation on your site.

The only people who will be able to endorse your skills are those that have a 1st level connection with you. This helps to weed out endorsements that are created by people who barely witness the actual skill. Make sure that you have enough 1st level connections to endorse you and that you can endorse to strengthen your profile.

LinkedIn skills and endorsements are another method of standing out. If used properly, it can establish a sense of expertise and credibility. It creates another way to connect with your friends, members, or fans. It can also be used to gain recommendations.

10. Use LinkedIn Ads and Sponsored Updates

LinkedIn sponsored updates publish our content to the news feed of all the members of LinkedIn. The ads are directed more towards a target audience and are posted in various areas of the site.

A sponsored update from LinkedIn is visible on all the different platforms. It is mobile capable. LinkedIn users are not able to opt out of seeing these sponsored updates. They can hide them, but not opt out. Therefore, the reach of the update is very beneficial.

Start creating your sponsored update by creating a campaign. Use the Campaign Manager and select "Create a business account" from the dropdown box. You can select the company you want to create a campaign for and name it. Click the "Create" button. To continue on with building your campaign, you must enter the billing information.

After the billing information is entered, you can go to your homepage and choose to create a new campaign. Select "Sponsor and update" and then click on the "Next" button. Follow the prompts through deciding how you want to narrow down your audience. Be careful not to be too selective on your audience. This may make your reach too small to benefit you. LinkedIn will allow you to target the location, company size, industry, job function or seniority.

Once the audience is selected, you can start determining your budget for the campaign. Consider paying when someone clicks on the ad or only when it has been viewed. Once you have finished, click on "Save changes".

You are able to narrow down your audience with creating an ad as well. Remember that targeting your audience helps to make sure that you are reaching the most beneficial of people. You do not want to keep it too lose or make it too tight. This may take some practice to find the right balance of selections that work for your business.

After creating an ad or sponsoring an update, you need to monitor it and make sure that it is working for you. LinkedIn will allow you to view the amount of interactions you receive from your post or ad.

A successful ad will need to land on a lead generating landing page. Your sponsored update should land to your business website. The ad is collecting leads for a specific product or service. Your ad should ask customers to perform a specific action. Ask them to fill out their contact information for more details. Tell them specifically what it is you want them to do. The ad should include an image that is bright and appealing. It should look good in 50x50 pixels. The ad should be refreshed monthly and monitored weekly.

LinkedIn does not have the same reach capability as Facebook. However, it is great at generating business to business interactions and establishing a more professional credibility. LinkedIn has a better chance of promoting materials with companies which is expected, rather than using a platform such as Facebook. Your LinkedIn ads and sponsored updates have the potential to target the perfect audience and build great connections with customers.

11. Find Sales Prospects with Linked In

LinkedIn is a social media website focused on the way people are linked together. You have your 1st level connections, 2nd level, 3rd, and so on. It's important to reach out at all levels when finding your business network. Every person that you connect with gives you hundreds of others to find a common interest or need.

LinkedIn can boost your sales in many ways. You can use your profile to ask people to perform a call to action. Include something in your summary that asks them to do what you want them to. You can share information regarding your attendance to events. The events may be pertinent to your industry and create connections with those that are also important to the industry. Your profile can keep you up to date with industry events if you connect to the right profiles. You will know when and where everything that is being talked about is happening. Can you really afford to miss out on those opportunities?

Find a plan that works for you in using your LinkedIn profile for its full capabilities in sales prospects. You can assign a certain day of the week for adding a specific amount of connections. Make sure that you find a way to actually connect with them, not just request their acceptance. Consider complimenting them on their profile or involvement in a discussion. Flattery is always a good way to start a relationship. Find a goal for the amount of groups you will join in a 30 day period. Your involvement should not stop with joining. Take the first 5 days and start a discussion each day in those groups.

There are applications on LinkedIn that can make your profile more humanized and enjoyable. Take a look at the availability and select some that work for your chosen industry.

There are many ways to connect with people on LinkedIn. It's important that the connection is real and not just an acceptance. It is commonly known that a person requires several interactions before they start paying attention to you.

Make those several interactions count. If you use LinkedIn the right way for your online business sales prospects, you will become visible and valuable to all of your connections.

LinkedIn is another social media site that has rules for using it correctly. It's easy to fall into bad habits that are hurting your business reputation instead of helping it. Knowing what NOT to do is one of the best strategies for gaining connections. Here is a list of what you should not do on LinkedIn.

1. **Do not leave your page without a picture.** There are many reasons why. Let's start with the first impression you are giving people. A profile without a picture is boring and lacks personality. This is not the vibe you want to send.

2. **Do not send connection requests using the default setting.** Spend a little time personalizing your connection request. Show that you care about people's connections and that you are doing more than just building up the number of connections you have.

3. **Do not skip on the summary of your profile page.** This is a great opportunity to place your online business's website. People like to look over this brief information to know whether it's worth sticking around or not. Make sure to make it something worth investigating.

4. **Do not have a profile page full of typos or grammar errors.** You want to let people know that you are professional and an expert. Typos and grammatical errors say something totally different. It makes it look like you did things in a hurry or that you do not know what you are doing. Check things over and make sure that your page is grammatically correct.

5. **Do not miss out on using LinkedIn Groups.**

6. **Do not forget to make yourself anonymous when searching through people's profiles.** If you happen to check out a person multiple times, it can really make people feel that you are creepy. They can see that you have viewed their profile.

7. **Do not have a profile page without recommendations.** These should be valid recommendations from people you know.

8. **Do not miss out on following the competition.** This will show you who is still there and who left. You can see different industry news that may be new to you.

9. **Do not share information that is irrelevant to your industry.** People are connected to you for a reason. Do not stray away from that reason.

10. **Do not forget to create a group for your customers to belong to.** Give them a place to be heard and feel that they are a part of something.

11. **Do not submit spammy messages into a discussion.** This will give a bad impression of your intentions.

12. **Do not over post.** You only need to post once a day. Anything more than that can become annoying.

13. **Do not insert negativity into a discussion.** People will steer away from you.

14. **Do not send spammy messages to your connections.** Remember that social media is meant for networking and not selling directly.

15. **Do not forget to create a unique URL for your LinkedIn page.**

13. Create a Pinterest Business Page

Pinterest is different from other social media sties. It focuses on visuals to grasp a following of individuals. The visual provided for products and information help people to remember what they see. Pinterest is geared more towards people interested in buying and accepting products and services rather than Facebook or LinkedIn which is more to do with connecting people.

By establishing a Pinterest Business page to help gain traffic to your website, it will promote your products and also establish connections with more people.

Start by clicking on the "Sign Up" tab.

Complete the profile information. Make sure you complete everything to take advantage of all the benefits of Pinterest.

Upload an image for your Pinterest account. Make sure that the image is attractive and looks good at small sizes.

Verify your website.

> Go to the settings page.

> Click on verify website.

> You are asked to download an HTML file which should be uploaded to your server.

> Pinterest will show a green checkmark next to your domain in searches for your business.

Once you have created your business page, incorporate different buttons and pins throughout your own website. This will help to complete your profile. You can use the "Pin It" icon for people to be able to post your items to their boards. There is a "Follow" button that will allow people to follow you on Pinterest.

Pinterest is all about being visually appealing. Your graphic should be interesting, so try and include your logo into your pictures. This will help increase your brand recognition. When followers "like", comment, or "pin" your picture, be social and respond. Thank them for the engagement.

Pinterest can help provide your business with a catalogue of your products and services. You can use the platform to reach out to those who may not stumble across your website. Let your website be the landing page for your pins. This will increase the traffic you get to your site.

14. Use Pinterest for Product Promotion

Pinterest is a great platform to pursue for product promotion. You can gain followers by showing the products you can deliver.

The images that you deliver are going to be what increases the followers. You have to make sure that the images are pleasant to look at and interesting. Consider having images of people using a product instead of the product by itself. Find a way to add information to the image to increase the recognition of your brand.

Your images should be grouped together on boards. Each board should have a different theme. Some use product color, others use size. You can create boards that display the most popular. You can showcase the products that are new.

Your products need to sell themselves through their display. Accompany any pictures with accurate and fun descriptions. Be careful not to pin every item you sell. Use the items as teasers and gain the traffic to your website. Encourage people to travel back to your site to see more of what you have to offer.

Pin your own products and share them with your followers. This will increase the visibility to your products. Make sure that your descriptions use keywords that make the product easy to search. If you are selling a service instead of a product, consider pinning samples of your work.

Pinning samples of your work will increase credibility for your work. Followers will be able to comment, recommend, and review your work. They will also be able to share your work with others. This will increase your brand recognition and word of mouth about your business.

Consider pinning products that would be complimentary to yours. It will help to show that you are a part of a whole community. You are not in the industry for only you. It shows that you are not someone on Pinterest just to gain followers.

These types of accounts are considered spam. The added pins may also increase viewing of your own merchandise.

Take into consideration if your product may be a great gift. Pinterest has an option to view gift options at a certain price point. When you add in your product, you can include it into that "gift" category. The price should be included in the description of the product.

Boards are the separation of items on Pinterest. When you pin products, you want to place them on boards to separate them into organized categories. This will help your followers to enjoy the viewing experience.

Keep the most relevant of your boards on top. This will help to show your followers exactly what they need to see right away. Your board should include a cover image that is relevant to the topic and appealing.

Coming up with the content to pin may require some creativity. Consider doing some research into your customers and other businesses to find out what they are pinning. The boards that you create should reflect upon the businesses values, culture, interests, products, and services.

When you are creating a board, give it a great name. Make sure that the name reflects the topic and makes it easy to search.

There are many different options for sorting things out onto boards. Some consider separating products by color. In some industries, this makes searching for items that the customer needs easier. Try and understand what your customer wants in narrowing their choices. Use these options as starting points for creating your boards.

When you are coming up with ideas for your boards, you may have to travel a little away from your own products. Stay in line with your overall topic, but consider a creative way to interest people in the topic further, then have them travel back to your website for products or further information. Consider some ideas, such as highlighting customers passions and interests. You can share videos. They can also be how to videos that coincides with your products or topic.

You can also keep your followers and viewers engaged by having a board meant for new releases or new services. This will help them to see how often you are attending to your Pinterest page.

To increase engagement with others on Pinterest, make sure to re-pin others. Do not make yourself come across as a spam page meant to only gain business for you. When you take the time to re-pin others, they may return the favor. Likewise, when someone views yours, you may want to check theirs out.

Building boards is all about being creative. There are no rules or boundaries. The most successful of boards always keep in mind that they need to stay visually pleasing. Understand the fonts and color palettes that you are selecting from and follow their ideas as a template for how you should create your own Pinterest board.

16. Use Pinterest to Hold Contests

Pinterest is a great way to hold contests. The contests help to build followers and encourage people to check out your Pinterest page. It's important to know the rules of Pinterest before you use a contest for your online business.

It is recommended by Pinterest that you hold contests that reward quality and not quantity. In order to make your contest user friendly, you will need to keep things simple. The contest should remain fun and useful. Make sure that the contest is easy to enter in to. Making it difficult will lessen the amount of response you receive.

There are some guidelines of what not to do when holding a contest. You should quote Pinterest as sponsoring your contest. The Pinterest logos and symbols should not be included in your promotional material for your contest. Do not require adding pins for the contest. You should also not require pins for entry into the contest. It's also important that you do not ask people to vote for the winner of your competition.

When you decide to start using a contest on Pinterest, start by identifying your goal. What do you need to designate this contest as a success? Do you want increased activity to your website? Would you like more followers? Once you have the goal of the contest, you can decide what kind of contest you want to have.

Your contest should be related to your goal. If you want more traffic to your website, award those that make their way there. Find a way to lead your viewers to a landing page on your website

Make sure that the prize is worthy. It should be related to your topic and the award should be in relative amount to the amount of work that had to be put in.

Create a pinnable image that you can use to get the word out there about your contest. It should be attractive and creative. Make it fun and useful to your topic.

Promote your contest. Send an invitation to those on your network and within other social media sites. Send invites to your friends and family. Consider posting an ad or investing in promoting your contest over the radio.

When it comes time to choose a winner, consider an outside source for selecting randomly if that's what you promised. Make sure that you pay out the reward as quickly as possible. Find a way to showcase your winners. Consider a blog post about the winner or a winner's board for ongoing contests. This will help to get great feedback and continual participation.

Creating a Pinterest contest is a great way for any online business that wants to work towards achieving their goals. It will increase visibility. The contest will help you create a fun relationship with your customers and followers. =You can gain brand recognition and have fun doing it.

Infographics are a way to visually give a person data or information. It provides the data in a clear format that is easy to ready and quicker to obtain. Pinterest is a social media website known for its visual appeal. Therefore, the combination is great.

Using visual aids to get a point across is great because people remember more this way. It is known that people have relatively short attention spans and that they pick up visual information faster and gravitate towards these features. It's easier for them to retain what they see in comparison to what they read. Therefore, you should consider relaying brand or industry information in an infographic to help engage your audience and allow them to retain that information.

Your infographic needs to capture the attention of viewers. It should be easy to read. It should pop out. It also needs to be visually appealing. Any data that is included in the infographic needs to come from a reliable source. Any sources should be cited appropriately. Be careful to limit the amount of text that you use. Brand any images with your business logo as well, because this will help to increase brand recognition.

If you decide to create your own infographic, there are steps to take you through the process. Start by deciding your topic. Keep it relevant to your business and industry. Make sure that the topic is interesting to your customers. Consider the design of the infographic. If you have trouble coming up with something, research what others are doing. You will need to know what icons, graphics, colors and shapes you want to use.

Your infographic should jump out at viewers and capture them. This will allow you to increase visibility to your Pinterest page. Tie the infographic to a landing page on your website to increase engagement and traffic to your website. The infographic should be creative. It should be easy for followers to share it. Consider what would happen if the infographic went viral.

If you are not sure how to create the infographic on your own, there are websites and tools available to help you. Here are some of the more common ones:

a. Easel.ly
b. Infogr.am
c. Venngage
d. Piktochart

If you create and pin the proper infographic, you have multiple benefits for your online business. You can increase traffic to your website. You will increase your brand awareness. Pinterest is a world of visual stimulation. Infographics provide your brand information and capture that visual aspect at the same time. It's a win-win situation.

Pinterest is different from other social media sites. It has the same goal of networking, but there are different rules that a user must understand. It's important to know the standard of conduct for each social media site. Not knowing is far too damaging to your business's reputation. Here is a list of things to avoid when using Pinterest...

1. **Missing the opportunity to include your business information.** Too often, users do not complete information regarding their business. They are missing the opportunity to attract customers to their websites.

2. **Creating a profile that is incomplete.** All of the fields on the Pinterest profile have a designated space. Leaving any of it blank can give an empty appearance on our profile. It can also leave out pertinent information that can be searched for by other users.

3. **Pinning items that are not worthy.** If you plan to pin something for everyone to see, make sure it is worth the space on your board and the time it takes to view it.

4. **Not following other businesses.** It's important to show that you are part of a community. If you are worried about getting followers and forgetting to show that others have something worth seeing, you will create a bad reputation for your business. Your presence can be seen as spammy.

5. **Pinning images for Google images.** It's easy to find pictures that you like on google images. However, you

will need to go back to the original source to pin them accurately.

6. **Abandoning your profile.** Make sure that your followers can count on you to update them regularly. Do not go a long time without posting or followers may become disengaged by your profile.

7. **Ignore your followers.** Giving positive feedback and acknowledgment helps to engage the audience. It will increase the word of mouth that you get and the amount of recommendations. When a person has a positive experience, they are more likely to share it.

8. **Leave a board description blank.** This is valuable real estate. You have the room to utilize 500 characters for your description. These words help to make your board searchable among other users. Take advantage of the opportunity and find the right words to make you pop up to the right customers.

9. **Leaving your company website out of your profile.** You have the opportunity to market your website and increase traffic. Use it. Consider adding the URL of your website into the "About" section. Find other places to include it. Your business website should be easy to find on your profile.

10. **Leaving empty space on your boards.** When you create a board, use the space. Empty space can give off the impression that is not complete. Therefore, viewers may move on. It may also seem that you aren't interested in your Pinterest community.

11. **Leave your account unverified.** Verifying your account increases your credibility. It also allows you to utilize analytics to see where you are doing well and need to improve.

12. **Using too much text.** Pinterest is all about being visual. Don't lead people away with too much text.

19. Create a YouTube Channel

YouTube is notorious for providing plenty of entertainment. It is the go-to social media on finding visual aids on any process. Consider using YouTube to help build your online business. You can use it to entertain, inform, or discuss your business, industry, or products.

To get started you will need to create a YouTube channel for your business. You will need to have a google account. Log in to your g-mail account with your user name and password. Go to "Create a new channel" on the YouTube page. Fill out the requested details completely. Missing any information may cause you to lose a connection. Click on the "About" tab. Go to the "Channel description" and enter the description of your brand. Click on the "Links" tab and enter the information to any other online profiles you would like to be connected to.

Once you have your channel completed and are happy with the display, you need to upload videos. Your first video should be a trailer for your channel. Let everyone know who you are and what it is you are planning on accomplishing. You will want to do some research regarding what others are doing. Take a look at the trends on YouTube and find out what everyone is viewing.

When you name your channel, make sure that you are using meaningful words. The name should include keywords that will make it easy for people to find your channel. Your channel will need to have information about your business website.

Your content needs to be interesting and relevant to your business. You should use high quality video. Keep your videos short and sweet. People do not have the attention span to stay connected for long amounts of time. If you have to have a lengthy video to get your point across, break it up into sections.

Since the idea behind social media is connecting with people, you have to find other people to connect with. Search out channels that are relevant to your topic and view their videos. Comment and ask questions when it is appropriate. Encourage them to view your channel. Go the extra mile to find the connections you need to get started.

Your YouTube channel will need to be goal oriented. If used correctly, you can spread word of mouth quicker and improve the ranking of your website and therefore it's possible to increase the amount of traffic to your business site.

YouTube is a great way to get your online business attention. Any social media site requires attention. Once you create your channel, you need to regularly update it. You will need to post regularly and interact with your community.

20. Create a Relationship between Your YouTube Channel and Your Website

YouTube has the capability to engage your audience in a great way. The visual aids help to keep their attention better than text. You can use interesting tactics to keep them focused. Since you have their attention, you will want to make good use of it. Make sure to keep your business website linked to your channel.

You can have the ending clip of your video be a call to action. This is a strategy where you tell people exactly what you want them to do. You will need to follow-up with how they need to do it and why. This is the easiest way to utilize the audience's attention.

You can also link your website to your channel on YouTube. You will need to go to the "Associated Websites" to connect videos to your website landing page. You can use that landing page to collect lead information, gather survey responses, or drive traffic to your website. This helps to keep your viewers engaged. In order to do this, you have to have your account verified. Go to the "Webmaster's Tools" and add your site as an associated website. YouTube will take you through the process of getting verified. Follow the steps. Once you are verified you can visit "Advanced Channel Settings". Add your website in the "Associated Website" section.

Linking your website to your YouTube channel is a great way to increase traffic and engage your customers, followers, and fans. You will change your viewers into visitors of your website.

21. Post Great Content on YouTube

The trick to getting the most out of your YouTube channel is the content that you post. You will need to keep in interesting. It's important to fill a void in your customer's lives. You will need to value quality over quantity.

Interesting content will need to be relevant to your topic. Your content should be unique. The first few seconds are the hook. The hook needs to grab the viewers. If they are not engaged in the first few seconds, they will stop watching. After the hook, you will want to find a way to continue engaging the viewers. Keep the video short. People have the attention span of 1-2 minutes. This is the amount of time that does the best on YouTube. If you have to lengthen the video, consider breaking it into sections.

When you are deciding what you want to talk about, keep your customers in mind. Your videos should aim at resolving a problem they may have. You may need an informative session. People often post how to videos. Consider showcasing products that you sell with real life examples of use.

Quality should be important in your video. You will want to be sure that you have the right amount of light. No one wants to strain to see details of the video. Your sound quality should be good. You will also want to eliminate any background noise that could be distracting. Many perceive a quality video as one that contains different transitions, overlays, and graphics. However, there is a danger in adding too many of these.

The video is an important part of your content, but it's also important to focus on proper descriptions. The words that you use in descriptions will help to make a viewer find you. The first couple of sentences are the only thing that is viewed on a search. Within those few sentences, you will want to include the most important keywords. There is also the option of labeling a video with tags. The tags have the same concept. You want to make sure that someone who may find value from your video is able to find it through a simple search. The tags that you select are what makes that happen.

It can seem very overwhelming to try and name your video. The best course of action is to keep your titles simple. This will help when they are getting searched. You will want to include keywords. For the sake of organization, consider including your brand name and an episode number. This will help you when referring to information.

Your YouTube channel needs content that is entertaining, informative, or educational. It should be relevant to your community. You will need to have great quality videos that answer problems customers may have. You will need to create the content in a way that makes it easy to find for viewers. All of these factors will determine if you are able to keep your audience engaged.

22. Using Transitions, Overlays, and Graphics in YouTube Videos

Getting your brand out to your followers may require you to find a way to get your logo or information present in another way. You can do that by installing overlays into your videos. You can also attract viewers by using great transitions and graphics.

Transitions are the means of getting from one setting to another in a smooth manner. There are many different options in video editing programs. A simple cut is very easy. It is going straight from one video to another. It has to be timed properly so that no important information is cut.

You can also use a dissolve transition. This is just as it sounds. The picture dissolves into the next scene. This is what most shows and movies use. It is so smooth that it usually goes unnoticed.

A light flash transition is more noticeable. It resembles the flash from a camera. As the scene ends, the screen will go white for a split second before commencing on the new scene. This can be good in moderation. Too much of it can be quite distracting however.

A particle wipe is very creative when done correctly. It is the removal of one screen and introduction to the next using bubbles, particles, or dust across the screen. It works best when the substance that is spread links to the topic being talked about.

Overlays are a good way of adding a message to your videos. When you add an overlay, a box will come up on the video as it is being played. You can use that area to ask for a call to action, relay details about the company or events, or to promote materials.

Graphics are great for videos. They help to build character and give your video personality. Adding graphics can make a video unique and fun. Consider building your own graphics or hiring someone to do it.

Annotations are a necessary part of any YouTube video. This is text written on the video itself. You can use them to direct viewers toward certain actions while viewing. Make sure that the annotations are not distracting to your video. People should like them, not yell at them. The annotations you add should add value to your video. They can include promotion material. They can be used to give your website information at the end of a video. They can also be used to separate parts with titles and headings.

Having great content is imperative to gain benefits from YouTube. Adding smooth transitions can improve the quality of your video. Overlays can help to provide information to your viewers. Graphics are a great way to build brand recognition and have fun. Finally, annotations are needed to give your video depth and quality. Consider how you can implement these features into your videos.

23. Build Your YouTube Community

YouTube is a social media site that utilizes videos. The idea behind it is to make connections and network. Therefore, to use YouTube as a tool to build your online business, you need to become a part of that community.

The best way to build your community is to have content that is valuable. If your content is addressing a problem within your customers, they will automatically travel to you through their search. You will have little to do. Your content will engage them and keep them asking for more.

The types of engagement that are important on YouTube are likes, comments, and shares. You want to receive as many of them as possible. You also want to give them to those that have relevant channels. This will help to increase the reach your business will have. It will also increase your visibility within the industry.

There are ways to call a fan to action. You can ask them for their opinions. Consider asking them to relay any questions that they have. A tactic that is commonly used is to ask for viewers to subscribe in the video that is posted. You can also increase your community be asking other channels to feature you. Consider featuring them in return. It will help to reach out to their followers and likewise for them.

If you are going to ask people to interact with your channel, you have to be prepared to do your part. You will need to respond. You will need to keep them engaged. Be positive in your answers and keep interactions light. If you keep interactions positive, people are more likely to share your channel.

Once you have established your brand and your style, try and stay consistent. A reliable community will start to tell you what you are doing right and what you are doing wrong. Schedule your up-loads. Your fans, friends, and followers should be able to count on you for new content.

A fun and entertaining way to keep your viewers engaged is to create a pay-off situation. Start by announcing how many followers you have. Let everyone know where you want to be in the future. Then, promise a fun task after seeing that goal reached. Announce through your videos where you are at in achieving that goal and remind them of where you want to be. Once you get to your goal, post yourself performing the task that was promised. It's a celebration of you, your community, and your goals. It can be silly, fun, rewarding, or just a great release for you.

Once you have the ideal relationships with your community, make sure to acknowledge them. You can give them a shout-out in your video. Find a way to acknowledge those that are contributing the most to your channel and acknowledge all others that participate.

YouTube is a huge community of potential customers. Take advantage of the relationships you build for marketing your online business. Find common connections and grow them with respect and acknowledgment.

Just like any other social media website, there are rules to joining the community. If someone enters the community and disregards these rules, they may ruin their reputation before they even begin. Therefore, as someone looking to build an online business, it's important to know the rules of YouTube. Here is a list of what to avoid:

1. **Using titles that already exist.** Do some research before uploading your content. Make sure that your title and descriptions are relevant and unique. Do not create a situation where you could be accused of plagiarism.

2. **Choosing quantity over quality.** It can be easy to start pushing more and more videos to keep a constant update. However, you need to make sure that all of your videos are of quality. If you need to update less often to keep the quality up, then do it.

3. **Forgetting hyperlinks in the description.** The description gives you an opportunity to promote your site and direct people to that. Use it. It will also help your business website with ranking.

4. **Long videos.** YouTube users like things short. Be careful not to include a lot of text. Keep things simple and short. Short videos will help to keep your viewers engaged.

5. **Forgetting the subscribe button after videos.** Use the opportunity of engaged viewers to gain a

larger following. The subscribe button offers a call to action.

6. **Forget to check out others.** If you have a channel that is one-sided, people will back away from you. They will think that you are spammy. It's important to give as much as you expect to get from the YouTube community.

7. **Being unrealistic.** We have all seen the videos that go viral. There are a lot of videos uploaded to YouTube every minute. Not every video that has the potential to go viral does.

8. **Posting content that is inconsistent.**

9. Ignoring the community. If the community has invested the time to try and interact with you, it's important to give the attention back. Ignoring them will only leave them feeling excluded and with a negative impression about your business and channel. Don't alienate the following you want by ignoring them.

10. **Omitting annotations.** Annotations are notes that are viewed on videos. They help to animate it.

11. **Posting a video that shows someone looking at the screen instead of the camera.** This goes into making sure that your video is of good quality.

12. **Omitting contact information.** The idea is to drive traffic to your business website. Post contact information whenever you have the opportunity.

25. Create a Twitter Profile

Twitter is a large community of social media users. It offers a platform for sending short messages and following those that you are engaged by. Every business should have a Twitter profile that compliments their style. The best profiles will grab people before reading the content. The content will seal the deal for followers and begin to grow a profitable relationship.

Start by creating your profile.

Go to twitter.com and click on Sign-up.

You will need to fill out your name, email address, and password.

A new screen will be displayed that allows you to enter additional profile information. Complete every area in entirety. Any blank sections will cause you to miss out on opportunities. When asked to enter the name you want to use, be selective. When people want to direct message you, your name has to appear in the message. It is part of the 140 characters that are allowed in a tweet – so keep the name short.

Click on create my account.

An email will be sent to the email address you first entered. Go to the email and open up the link. The link will verify your account.

Start adding additional profile details. On the right side of the screen, you will see the option to edit the profile.

Start with placing photos to the profile. There are 2 that need to be uploaded. The profile pic is small. It will appear as an icon in most places. The second picture is the header picture that appears on your account. Make sure that your pictures are relevant to the audience you are trying to attract and that they're good quality.

Next, you will want to complete your bio information. This is your opportunity to grab viewers. Wow them with a humanized description of your business. Be sure to include a link to your website. Keep the description short and sweet, but interesting.

You have the opportunity to customize your background. Use the opportunity to create brand recognition. Consider placing your logo or your company name throughout the background to capitalize on the prime real estate of your account.

Finally, check your security settings. There is an option to protect your updates. As a business, looking for more connections, you do not want to do this. People should be able to see your content. That's the purpose of this strategy.

26. Build a Team of Twitter Followers

Twitter is a social media site that has the potential to reach a huge number of people. It would seem that the best tweeters would be those with the biggest numbers. This is not always the case. People can see how many followers you have and who they are. As a business, your Twitter account is defined by your followers and your content.

The best way to build a community of followers is to go out hunting for people worthy of your following. The idea is that they will see a returned value in your Twitter account. You want to avoid a community of people that are ignoring your content and not participating in your conversations. The idea behind creating content that is engaging is to deliver it to people that will continue to be engaged by it.

Find the influencers in your industry. These can be names that you are familiar with. They may be people with a way of words. These influencers have a talent at getting people to follow through on a call to action. If they believe that a story is interesting and ask their community to check it out, their followers will. They will also take the time to comment on the story and keep the participation going. They show that they have a place in that community.

People will not follow you on Twitter if they do not know you are there. You have to make your presence known. You can link your other social media sites to your Twitter account. Include your presence on Twitter in emails or on your website. Tell the world where to find you.

Create a Twitter profile that showcases why people should follow you. Declare yourself an expert and let everyone know what you have to offer. People don't know that you do well at your job if they just met you. You have to clue them in on your capabilities and talents. Use the bio section to let people know about the company's values, products, services, or interests. If they have a connection between that, they may become interested in following you.

Your content is important to creating and keeping a following. The content should be consistent in topic and be posted regularly. Use hashtags within the content to let people know your topic. Consider keywords for your hashtags that make it easier to search your material when people are looking for it.

Search for others using the same hashtags you are, as there is already a common ground. See if their page has regular postings and interactions within the community. Consider following them and introducing yourself. Become a part of their community and they may support you in your own.

Once you have followers, find out who they are following. Spend some time searching for the right people to follow to build reputation and credibility to your own Twitter account. Send out compliments to people where they are deserved. You can acknowledge who you are speaking to with an @ symbol before their user name. Compliments provide a positive interaction with a person, making them more likely to want to connect with you again. It's the best way to keep things on a good note and promote them wanting to engage in conversation with you again. It also shows common interest in things. For example, if you let someone know that an article they shared was awesome, they will instantly understand that you have something in common.

The idea behind Twitter and using it to grow your business network is to find followers that are going to spread the word. This means that you want them to share your tweets, retweet, comment, like, or mention your business. You will need to find the people that are willing to do the job for you. You can build a community of 3,000 people and have no success without interaction. It's not the number of people you find, there are millions that are easy to find. It's about finding the right ones, which may take some work.

Use Twitter to spread the word that you are the expert of your industry. Show people that you are interested in more than just selling your product or services. Invite them into your world and dive into theirs as well. You will be rewarded with success when you connect with the right ones.

27. Create the Perfect Content on Twitter

Using Twitter to boost your online business requires followers that are engaged. You have to find these followers through interacting with them on their own pages and through creating great content for you page. There are many different ways to find great content. The bottom line is you want content that is going to attract people with common interests. You want to find topics that will spark discussion and keep people talking and coming back for more.

Start finding the right content by monitoring the market trends. You should know what is coming up and what is phasing out. Incorporate those trends into your tweets. Look at different events that may be occurring in your industry. Find new products or services that will benefit your followers. Talk about your experience with those products or ask about their experience.

Your tweets should be interesting. The easiest way to gain followers is to grab their attention. If you found the right audience, tweets that teach something are beneficial. People generally want to get better at what they do. Creating tweets that help them achieve that may prove positive for them and get them wanting to follow you for more.

Create content that makes people smile. It will be more memorable. Consider sharing good news. You can congratulate someone within your Twitter community. Try and make them laugh with jokes that surround the industry. Be careful not to offend or hurt anyone's feelings. Make sure that the jokes are professional.

Find a way to solve your customer's problems. Posting the solution or ideas that could help the matter will make them consider a tweeting relationship with your business. You will be building a reputation as an expert on the topic and open the door for future questions or comments regarding other problems. It increases engagement with your followers.

Fill your content with appropriate symbols and signs. The # sign is used to note keywords or topics that can be searched for. Using the right keywords will make your tweets reach out to a larger audience. They are viewed by your followers and people following those keywords. People searching the keywords will be able to find your tweets. You can speak about or to someone using the @ symbol before their user name. This is called a mention. When you want to send a message directly to a person, you start your tweet with "DM@user name".This will send a private message to them alone.

The idea behind your tweet is to expand your audience with retweets, mentions and conversations. Focus away from promoting your product and more on building your audience. Add in images. You should use attractive and high quality images ieally, to attract people's attention.

It's also important that you post your content regularly and consistently. Know enough about your audience to understand what times are not beneficial. If most of your audience works from 8 to 5, these hours should be off limits. You also want to be sure to post 5-10 times each day to grab enough attention.

Your content is important to attracting the right audience. You will want to keep things fresh and be creative. Include images. Keep your words positive and uplifting. Know how to use Twitter appropriately and you will gain its full benefits. With all these tactics in your back pocket, your Twitter audience will quickly grow to a valuable community that supports your online business.

28. Use Twitter Advertising

Twitter has the ability to further your marketing for your online business. There are 3 different ways that you can set up Twitter to assist you with this. Keep in mind your budget and what you are trying to accomplish with your ads.

A Promoted Account is just as it sounds. You will pay Twitter to place your account in the suggested box of those within your niche. It will help to make you visible to a large selection of those in your industry. This can increase your following, traffic and improve brand recognition.

A Promoted Tweet is where Twitter is inserting your tweet into the feed of those that meet the criteria. On a normal basis, your tweet is only viewed by those that are following you. This option extends the reach and builds your audience. You are asked to pay for this service when someone interacts with the tweet. They need to comment, retweet, or message you about the tweet itself.

A Promoted trend places you on the top trending list. This is a pricey option for advertising. It reaches out to a more general crowd of people.

Start a new advertising campaign by signing into Twitter Advertising.

Click on "New Campaign".

Choose a promoted tweet, account, or trend.

Fill out the questionnaire provided regarding your brand. Complete it entirely and as detailed as possible. These questions will help to find those that are in your niche.

Select options to target your audience with. You can choose keywords, television, or interests.

Decide and enter your budget for the ad.

Select and complete your method of payment.

Your ad campaign is created.

When you use promoted tweets, it's important to use content that is great. It should be engaging. Consider adding your website address into the message. You may want to start a contest, or share a coupon for a valuable or popular product, or ask a question. Whatever will keep the followers active is what you want to do.

Twitter has its own unique language. There are people out there that are masters of the Twitter community. If you are new, it's important to know what not to do. Doing the wrong thing can give your business a bad reputation and hurt your networking capability. Here's a list of what to avoid:

1. **Not using your background.** This is free real estate for you to build brand recognition. Take advantage of the opportunity and make the most of it. You should make your background attention grabbing and unique and tailor it to match the style of your business.

2. **Not being active on Twitter.** People want to follow you for a reason. They don't want silence. Find the content that will keep them wanting more and get it out there regularly. If they are able to trust that you will be posting useful information on a regular basis, they are more likely to recommend others to follow you. Seeing your Twitter handle often will help to keep your business fresh in their mind.

3. **Tweeting too much.** There's a point where too much talk becomes annoying. You don't want the Twitter community to ignore you because your messages are becoming too frequent. Too many messages drown out the meaning of one single message. You lose the power behind what you are saying. You will also lose traffic and followers.

4. **Talking all about you.** Self-promoting can be very bad on social media. It's ok in small doses and done at the appropriate times. Constant promotion can come

across as pushy. People will be less likely to follow you and have less interest in what you have to say. They will feel like every message has an ulterior motive of collecting their money. Keep tweets limited to 5-10 a day.

5. **Not checking your tweets before posting them.** Proofing your tweets is important and shows the level of professionalism in your business. It's also important that you review your tweets for any upsetting information of miscommunication of ideas before they are posted.

6. **Tweeting the same thing in the same day.**

7. **Auto DM people after they follow you.** This is annoying to people. It is not needed to reach out to everyone that has followed you. If they see content that engages them they will interact on their own.

8. **Auto-follows.** Handpick your audience to get the best results out of your Twitter strategy.

9. **Making tweets too long.**

10. **Mass retweeting.** This is too impersonal. It will alienate your followers. Consider commenting instead of retweeting everything you like.

11. **Begging for followers.** This is a cheap trick that looks awful for a business. Find your audience in a credible way. Use great content and engaging conversations to get followers instead.

30. Consider Using a Social Media Manager

Sometimes you may read all the details and realize that your business definitely needs a place in the social media world. However, you may not have the skills or time to complete the tasks that are needed. You don't have to back away from the idea. You can hire a social media manager to keep your business benefiting from social networking.

A social media manager is responsible for creating content. They should have experience in copywriting, design, and creativity. The right person can create wining content that will lead to more clicks and leads for your business.

Find a manager that can analyze the market. They should understand the need for experimentation and analyzing data. Once the data is gathered they need to present it in a way that everyone can understand and use. This will help to keep your business creating new and effective strategies for your social media campaign.

It's important for anyone managing social media for a business to stay current. There are people out there with a thirst for news. They have to know everything that is going on. Finding that person will help you to keep up with trends and increase your traffic.

A social media manager needs to be a customer service rep for your business. They should be able to handle positive and negative feedback in a way that matches the values of your business. This will help you to keep the traffic you worked so hard to gain.

A large community needs to be facilitated to the best of one's ability. The proper manager will know how to be resourceful. They will stimulate discussions and connect people. This will increase the amount of engagement from your social media sites.

There are many places to find your social media manager. Consider LinkedIn, Twitter, Mashable or Media bistro. Ask them questions related to your topic and make sure they can handle themselves. Throw situations at them and make sure that their style matches the values of the company. Go with your gut and find the person that best fits into your company. A social media manager can be very profitable for an online business in the long term.

When things get overwhelming, your social media accounts may begin to be left behind. If you are having someone else manage them, you don't have to worry about this. It's important to address the issues, even if you aren't the person that can do it. Find the right person and get the job done. Your business can't afford to miss out on the opportunities that social media provides.

Conclusion

Social media is needed to reach out to a larger audience. Your business needs to embrace social media and find the right strategy to gain success. Finding the right strategy will benefit your business in the form of increased sales, loyal and repeat customers and brand recognition. Your social media marketing will help to cut costs on additional advertising.

Social media marketing for your online business is too big of an opportunity to pass by. If you find a working strategy, you will be hosting discussions that are valuable to your industries. The right strategy will be keeping your business up to date on current trends. You will find a way to target customers that would otherwise never be within reach of you. The possibilities are only as limited as your strategy.

These thirty strategies are just the beginning of a very profitable marketing strategy. There is more to be found. New techniques and strategies are being created every day. As networks are created and changed, so are the strategies. As a business, you will need to find the strategies that work for today, but also research what will work for tomorrow. Stay consistent but relevant to today's audience.

Pick the strategy or strategies that work for your business and boost your business. Create an expert reputation that will follow you throughout. Combine different strategies to come up with one of your own. Bust most importantly, remember to have fun and enjoy it – social media marketing is most successful when you enjoy it!

Thank you for taking the time to read this book. I hope you enjoyed it. If you did, I would appreciate if you could leave an Amazon review, as that would greatly help self-published authors such as myself.

www.ingramcontent.com/pod-product-compliance
Lightning Source LLC
Chambersburg PA
CBHW061031050326
40689CB00012B/2762